POEMS
ABOUT SILENCE

Other Continuum Books by
EDWARD BUTSCHER

Sylvia Plath: Method and Madness

❧ POEMS ❧
ABOUT SILENCE

Edward Butscher

A Continuum Book
THE SEABURY PRESS
NEW YORK

THE SEABURY PRESS, INC.
815 Second Avenue
New York, N.Y. 10017

DESIGNED BY NANCY DALE MULDOON
Printed in the United States of America

LIBRARY OF CONGRESS CATALOGING IN PUBLICATION DATA

Butscher, Edward.
  Poems about silence.

  (A Continuum book)
  I. Title.
PS3552.U85P6   811'.5'4   75-34346
ISBN 0-8164-9278-6

FOR PAULA
La belle dame avec amour

CONTENTS

7

MOTHER AND CHILD

PERSONAE

THREE THEORIES OF FIELD COMPOSITION

PREFACE

PREFACES to volumes of poetry seem to have disappeared along with Walt Whitman, the rhythm method and great white whales. Theories died, and reason itself is suspect at the moment. Suffering in its purest, most personal state appears the only common poetic goal. Perhaps the loss of a godhead made such a response inevitable, the necessary purgation in fire before another self could be formed, but the time has certainly come for the poet to look beyond the self-indulgent anguish implicit in such an aesthetic.

Structure *is* meaning.

And poetry must return to design, however spontaneous, complex, full of surprises, without losing passion, if it is to make a recovery. The age dictates that these structures be erected upon the skyscraper heaps of bones left behind by the relentless "progress" of our civilization, but the poet himself is bound by no preconceptions as to the limits or worth of either despair or heroism, except with regard to the moral force always innate in literature.

More than ever, I believe, the poet has to accept both his wound and his bow.

11

ACKNOWLEDGMENTS

Acknowledgment is made for permission to reprint: Two lines from "Legend," from *The Collected Poems and Selected Letters and Poems of Hart Crane*, reprinted by permission of Liveright Publishing, New York; copyright © 1933, 1958, 1966 by Liveright Publishing Corp. Excerpt from "What Can I Tell My Bones?" copyright © 1957 by Theodore Roethke in *The Collected Poems of Theodore Roethke*, reprinted by permission of Doubleday & Company, Inc. Three lines from "from *The Black Book* (iii)," reprinted with the permission of Farrar, Straus & Giroux, Inc., from *Short Poems* by John Berryman; copyright © 1958 by John Berryman.

"Arctic Grace," "The Bench Sayer," "Passage to Manhattan" and "Still Life" originally appeared in *New American Poetry*, edited by Richard Monaco (McGraw-Hill), while various other poems from this collection first appeared in *The Little Magazine*, *Wisconsin Review*, *Poetry Northwest*, *Inlet*, and *Bacchy*. To the editors involved I extend my deep appreciation.

E. B.

✣ POEMS ✣
ABOUT SILENCE

As silent as a mirror is believed
Realities plunge in silence by . . .

—HART CRANE

OVERTURE

Silence sits
like a single sneaker
on my heart,
        so
        vacant
of the fisted, shot-sudden shout
that used to thrust it
against asphalt
slabs of sky,
        when
          closet night
could barely contain
my naked, hairless
chest refrains,
and every morning
was breakfast,
          then,
          always,
it could tongue
at will (whose?
impossible to know)
black umbrella trees
and tapestry
gardens,
      tap
      dancing
on my sister's
pebble grave.

But now
its laces trail waste
across my mind

like snails
on jeweler glass.

USED UP

I

His lips
speak braille.
       His breath whistles
      from my wheezing nose,
             each breath another song,
             each hair another hidden harp.

II

Sitting at a bare desk,
confronted by things, space
        around things,
        the taste of thought,
             the thick touch
             of my lard tongue,
       until one memory
       becomes many,
            then none,
            swallows sense.
It is dawn or dusk now.
Someone has died, been born.
        Silence is such
        that it replaces space,
             builds white walls
             around the mind,
      muffles eyes,
      muffles ears,
          in an asylum
          of lost selves.

III

But the abhorred vacuum
shapes a mouth to engulf words
              like stale
              potato chips.
                        Its crunching could be bones
                        or old teeth or cereal charms,
because there is
no difference,
              except in degree,
              swift atom shifts
                        between life
                        and blank wood,
                                  cherry soda,
                                  sweet blood,
                                            a dead boy's
                                            Kabuki mask.

DELIVERANCE

Silence comes once a day
like the milk man
or the mailman
or the woman
down the hall
who feeds on cockroaches.

You don't believe me?
Feel my heart smashing its
head against the bars
like an ape man
or a mad man
or the woman
down the hall
who sweeps out my cell.

I can hear it distinctly,
the rattle of disease
like milk bottles
or mail slots
or the woman
down the hall
ripping her skin into rags.

Listen to me!
That bitch always lies.
Ask the milk man
or the mailman
who carts my poems
like scum-stiffened sheets
past her damned door
everyday.

Don't be afraid of me.
I'm harmless, a child
with a telegram tongue
who spits out periods,
nothing at all
like the woman down the hall
whose cunt
chews men like candy.

GENESIS

When I was a child
my father sold my tongue
to a pawnshop
for three golden balls
and a ticket to Roseland.

The tomatoes are singing!
Each step takes ten
along the cement furrow.
I sit and count the hairs
on my dead dog's breath.
A tree (perhaps an extinct
elm) holds me tightly.

I squeeze her breast
and Wagner marches out
(that Nazi bastard!)
all the old beerhall songs,
her Jewish nipple kneeling,
keening, *mea culpa.*

The cat's silence
is fatal,
           motored
by a need
for mouse-swift grins,
fading into the television
set's sullen mask.

Her delicate belly button
opens pages of alien
signs, bent young men
in cassock shrouds, women
like grocery sacks.

Green leaves grow bugs,
devour the blank picture.
I feel the furry feet
of each pregnant cloud.
Winds rise like ghosts
to disarrange a skeleton.

Rusty with foreign blood,
the bayonet of me
enters
her slit-open field
to lick
at the foetus
of a dreaming skull.

ITSELF

Silence surrounds the skull
like a cotton dressing,
cleansing the mouth's
ragged army
of wounds,

soaking up my eyes until
their pupils shrivel
into prunes, lose
their pits
to a scalpel
twilight.

I lie in a field of lilies
like an earthquake
crater, a slash
of black air,
only air,

and a bottle of ink drops
from the mind, sits,
snug as an Indian
icon, upon
my navel.

*How many children
can a stone bear?*

Eyes popping like corks,
necks unwinding, splitting,
hearts slashed open to surprise,

ask the creepers and crawlers
underneath, who weep and

eat each other's tails
before the rainbow
garrotes them
in silence.

It's icy, flatter than a dime,
and look where it licks
my stomach bare
of doubting
hairs!

*How many stones
can fill a field?*

Ask the lovers knotted
in a scarf of naked
arms and legs,
shaking dust
from weeds,

one on top of the other,
on top of the other,

and so on
and so on

ISHMAEL

Sculptured from ice,
silent saints glow-grow
with dinosaur grins
inside my museum eye,

tears torn by glass
walls into a denial,
naked of everything
but their gauntness.

I hack at a frozen sea
and break into the tree,
riding its white ark
down coal corridors,
reeking of bull turds
and dry menstrual wine.

Screams of seaweed dull
headless antlers, soften
my search for the bud
of fermenting silkworms:

where rocks grow rocks
like carnival strippers
in an endless grind.

I float into a palace
of copulating wrecks,
ripped turrets, limp
guns, all rusting
in a coral grimace

at the way the eels
bite off a girl's
wedding ring finger,

and cross the tundra
of her ravaged corpse
to tear at her womb
like a dragon myth,
until eggplant seeds
explode its heart.

Seasons despair of sky,
and octopus laces lash
the infant crab roots
as gypsy jelly fish
wrinkle my stare,

licking air into jewels
that dance on the wind
like fossil stars.

GRANDFATHER

The autism of a wind-struck tree
lost amid
       some stark winter scene
       foreign to my city mind
       was its essence,
etchings of crippled spider limbs
that could
       have so easily been
       frames of skyscraper eyes
       studying
where night began and horizons
expired.

Silence was, first, a grandfather grace
and curse,
       a containment of world
       in a pipe bowl
       rusty from use,
scarlet, at times, with recalled passion,
steaming
       against the rimed
       porch windows,
       not in protest
       but relief,
a continuing of breath and brain after
life closed,

and, at other times, following a violent
coughing fit,
       when blood bubbled
       into a hot ball
       of foam fear,

shaky fingers tamped the wooden womb
frantically,
>tap-tap, tap-tap, tap-tap,
>as if will alone
>could win back
>all his lost continents.

My head ached with these silences and
tappings,
>the long pauses in between,
>and I felt his slow sap
>streak from my own ears.

GRANDMOTHER

No grandmother ever believes in silence,
perhaps out of fear,
           smearing the sky
           with offal
           curses,
or obsolete faith,
           kneeling in cement
           until knee-caps
           crack open.

The smooth wooden spoon stirred tomatoes
into an aria that flooded my mouth,
chunks of chopmeat and sausages
adrift like ravaged barges
in the lava sea
           that moved under her touch
           with long Satanic purrs,
           bubbling perfume
           fat promises.

But her chocolate eyes lied to me, brooks
of ice cream in a vast desert, as she
babbled about Michelangelo
on his back,
           below heaven,
                painting
the silence of fingers
that never touched
in a church where men
poisoned chalices,
slept with nuns.

Gold flaked from her palms, revealing
an open wound, and her eyes scabbed
over into dull brick,
                    fluids seeping
                    from her dry body,

She beat me with her walking stick,
mad as a miser whose horde has gone,
and the spoon remained in the pantry,
alone and sad, masturbated by darkness,
rusting to sand, then dust.

This is the second silence, she should have
whispered to me,
                    Gesù,
before she left,
                    a bundle of elbows and legs
                    carried out like trash
                    for burning.

OATH

My mind keeps hived
     the memory of accountant fathers
clutching sons to their vests
     like found gold,
mothers stumbling
     in a wing-hazed daze over
daughters' unborn breasts,
     silent, so silent
     under whip and prod,
except for their whispering feet,
feet like slippered leaves.

Is this the abyss of toothless mouths
that yawns whenever my foot starts
to swing away from itself,
searching another road?

Such silence closets mine
     and yours (not their's),
the hushed marble walls
     of a mausoleum in Queens,
the profound shushing sigh
     that haunts every hospital hall
where fear closes pores,
     has sap enough to muffle
each timid step
towards the last dark cell.

Perhaps. Perhaps not.
     It could simply be
a child's sucked-blunt pebble
     trapped in my intestinal maze,
a profane pit of fruitless malaise
     left over

from an undone feast
        when sorrow still had
        a honey-glaze of glory
to it that could mirror,
at will,
        its whole apple-small world.

But the silence
        must always be more, more than
an elm tree seen through glass,
        quick-witted limbs
spreading themselves
        under sea and seasonal wind,
more than a shabby dog
        lost among its cliff
        clenching toenails, who
lifts one leg from the trap release—

before trotting off its tail.

MOTHER

A specimen of barroom silence
carved out of melted
bathroom walls
by a boy's
      beery kisses,
      the will
            to power smoke,
            oval, dough-vague
                        forms rustling
                        on silken beds.

Pig knuckles float in her breasts,
move aside when I grip
those carnation cheeks
into tears,
      strange flesh
      of a stranger
                impressing me
                (for a moment)
                        upon
                        her altars.

There is death in there, I howl
through nipple slits,
lapping up her cream
excess as if it
      were my own,
      my own death
            blooming
            in the dark
                  each time
                  we emerge.

Who is this priestess who carries
voodoo dolls of me around
inside her cave's
coven cries
          for moon nails
          to hammer close,
                    saying nothing
                    to the treasures
                              I heap
                              at her door?

BUDDHA

He speaks spiders
to the thumb sausage
hidden below his
enormous appetite,
content that silence
can make even bone
come alive in pain
of a mocker's knees.

His altar is ancient
slabs of a made self,
flesh of gray stones
that leak lime blood
under my forehead's
relentless blows

as I rock with joy
before its Oriental
stare (mortared grim),
pulling wool clouds
from his grotto core
for another infant
to cat-cradle whole.

But pure sacrifice
does not dissolve
the knot mystery of
why sane men once
had to sniff fire
sipping human hair

or why only a son
could fill a lamb
with blood enough
for his own father
to spill, to lap up
like a rabid mutt.

HISTORY

I stay silent and age still
inside this abandoned sack,
poised, always, at the edge
of violence, a vicious line,
explosions of quicksand
sucking space blind.

The nun had slapped me hard
more than once, tears of pity
pure as bubbles in her eyes,
until her own blood rose like
a secret tide to swallow
my moon cheeks,
                    but air alone
can drown the wild kittens
of my lungs in furry waves,
in waves of women, in seas
and seasons without
shore or leaf.

The eraser was a hand-grenade
that struck the girl's high
cheek bone, blasting it
into chalk, parting her
face down the middle
like Gibraltar's cliffs.

Birds drop their eggs in her
mind where they breed larvae
that feed on her as she chokes
ah swoons into crooked *n*'s
and *w*'s, racked by her
mouth's rotted roof.

Sister, sister,
forgive me for not forgiving
your baby death, the coughs
I sucked in and spat out
like pieces of ash sky.

FATHER

Portraits in pearl
(pure as new soap)
decapitate the wall,
split by atomic art.

They remember self
as a sidelong glance
at the painted ship
where giants heaved.

Barrels of oil (still
warm as blood) heated
their hearts to steel,
kept thighs eel-white.

The sun refuses them
a moment's reflection,
gauze curtains like
shrouds over tusks.

But air respects air,
stands stiffer than
a mast before their
Egyptian profiles.

I honor all dust and
grasp their Spartan
spear-sperms to me,
laughing back at them.

ABELARD

A sliver of ice-water slices
my tongue,
  and you are there
  again (never here)
     before my empty lips
     can rim the cracked mug,
brimming blood stares
at the brink of a vision,
    a girlish hand, circlet
    of snow that restores
       my dangling,
       poker-hot tongue,
melting in your marsh
mouth like my lost
   penis (Plato's perfect
   light cupped to a sun)
      those first
      holy nights.
The bells of your laugh break
at my feet,
  and you are here
  again (never there)
    as I sprawl in clownish
    disarray before our son,
(cap in hand)
a cupless beggar
   mumbling curses
   like prayers
    at the grave of you
    between my legs.

RITUAL

Three women drift through me,
three paint rags
igniting straw hands
like torches,
burning air to smoke
that makes the walls swell,
sweat themselves alive.

The silence is never still,
least of all
when I remember
to hang up my clothes,
drink milk from a glass.

Cockroaches pour out of cracks
in my blossoming palms,
fly like squadrons
of Japanese suicides
at my eyes,
clogging my throat
with mobs upon mobs
of screaming, writhing leaves.

Three women crawl from me
and swirl naked
under the kitchen bulb,
their gray braids unloosening
like fragile fans,

their wrinkled faces
falling into mine.

MARRIAGE

The curtains rustle near
your bed like whispers
of hidden rapists.

You listen too hard and soon
their secrets are yours,
from the old ghetto:

Jews in knots, black hats,
beating their women
for having Rachel braids,
hair that flames in a river,
flowing with milk flesh
around their dreams.

The second ulcer bites home,
nurses the first,
                              husband
of stone turning
your intestines
into snakes.

You feel your mother's mad
screams like cancer
fists in your
breasts,
bunching,
unbunching,
bouquets of iron,
candy-store grates
screeching into place
with a subway's solitude,

and you listen too hard
to a clock that ticks
with your father's
patient heart

before it flutters
like a gull on a hook,
before it flies away, leaving
behind a trail of blood
like tainted coins.

Listen to me, my love,
my kiss of silence
upon your lips
like a hymn.

SELF-PORTRAIT

He scratches his balls
with one secret hand
while the other reaches
deep into space (past
comets) to stroke the sun
awake, to stir the night
like a peasant stew.

Brother, friend, fellow drunk,
whose life has a meaning yet,
tattered and tottering
at the top of the stairs
before plunging into a swamp's
slime to rescue Atlantis
from the muddy margins
of birth and death,

I love your eyes, so brown,
so wide in perpetual surprise
at what your purse lips
can really swallow,
gnaw, bundle into colors
raw as exposed wires.

His mind fumbles ideas
like a pocket of coins,
their glitter bursting
free of ordinary cloth
in touches of a sunset
that leaks white greed
like a bovine smile.

Corruption without extremes
in a Dutch balancing of dams,

45

corruption your face has
known and loved like scarlet
rivers of a virgin's ruin,
belching arias where light
carries melody to its
sweet cherry excess,

melting skin at every
bone-stitched seam
until sin itself can heal
all breaks,
         and babies
grow like roses
in old burghers' cheeks.

IN MEDIAS RES

Like a rose swallowed by a crystal ball,
perfect silence is always imagined.

Why had I thought of Jewish children
when I stared at the winter oaks this
morning,
                grown gaunt against gray skies?

Outside the window, the birds nudge
and threaten one another aside
from the sunflower seeds
I spread on the lawn,
black birds, large as rooks, sleek
as wet macadam, flowing over all,
sparrows like hyenas darting in
to steal a half-gnawed shell,
an occasional cardinal
stopping for his dole,
a kiss of obeisance
from a plain wife.

Planets, seas, children,
nothing can contain their motion
or bring back a single leaf.

After the war, like vomited debris
caught in another tide, they tumbled
back into the bracken sea of Europe
or rode the current of a mindless urge
to the land where Christ, rabbi to their
worst nightmares, was slaughtered
by well-meaning Americans.

Count the ticks in a clock
that swings between battery
extremes of antique beliefs.

I feel secure as dusk approaches slyly,
certain, oddly delighted, while they peck
the concrete earth apart and pull
the winter grass (mustard-gas yellow)
into pieces of straw for the air
to reap,
   splitting a nut like an oyster
for the succulent foetus within,
discarding shells and images
of other shells.

Neither Jewish nor old enough
to have fought or felt the terror
of a discovery out of time,
        I had made
masks out of fallen leaves,
       face
upon face of cartoon anguish,
collapsed cheeks, eyes, mouths,
pivoting in a whirlpool of pity and wind
that ripped my breath away.

Perfect silence is a poem before sleep
like a shack around my squatting mind.

CELEBRATION

If I had a son,
a chubby boy with glasses
and a shy grin
who giggled at my jokes,
I would clasp his hand
each night until
it hurt,
or kill him
        (if I could)
with a sudden fist
between his eyes,

to see, to be
the point of the flat
bright world
that tilts our teeth
downward.

Balance
        (I would will
him still)
           is the pin crux
of it,
    a flair
for remembering which
razor end can be
held close
to slit the owl's lid
without a chance
of paring thumb
from bone,

to see with,
my son,
marble light
pure as a moon cry.

ARTIFICE

The house curtains silence
of eighty-eight years,
a rich man's cottage
where his little girl
(an only child)
once drew
crayon tigers
on the bedroom wall,

where the sea
roars across a moor
of bloody hares
and fish-skeleton pines,
roars, roars, roars,
but recoils from the threat
of my profile's
jagged blade.

It was built for luxury's sake,
and escape
from the city's sweaty
cells, lined with books
and a white fire place
of autumn leaves
that kept
night at bay.

Porches, upstairs and down,
wavered in the heat
of adults
laughing like flames
behind their white
columns, dancing
moon to moon,

until the paint peeled back
from oaken bone
like lips from fangs,
and the wind crashed home,
drunk, clawed without
pity or hope
at the bolted French doors.

The dark floors are still
polished to a wicked
gleam, burnt
almond,
and dull merchant
portraits still sit against
the tide
of a declining fortune.

The kittens curled
in the candelabra jars
were half-asleep
when the long tigers
began their slow descent,
the little girl
like butter
in their mouths.

JESUS

An uprooted finger
clenched like a slug,
I cannot believe in myself,
am a deity of palm trees
taking root in sand,

a beaten donkey
for carting kings
across the bare backs
of their sweating slaves,
a carrion-carrying crow
clawing at the sun's
entrails for signs
of dove grace.

I feel real enough,
weep myself asleep
under lashes
of beasts,
cut myself on soldier swords
gashing out hearts
of steel men,

even the agony of daisies
yanked from their mothers'
Egyptian arms wounds me,
                              makes me
scream like a hare.

I punish flesh to own my own,
Magdalen's breasts supporting
my vaulting, vaunting dream
as I enter her silent
garden of muddy beds

and fallen garlands,
a god at last.

I will not live by the old law,
nor will I love by the new,
kneading myself into less,
but softer,
        tender as a leaf
for old gums
to masticate.

Whipped,
        I do not cry out,
spat at like a whore,
        I smile back at them,
the multitude of loaves
and fishes
who urinate in my face.

I am the bastard son
whose blood
freshens ashes,
makes deserts bear fruit,
corpses rise again,

but I love life
more than death,
        sweet Magdalen,
finger me home.

LUCIFER

The brown puppy hitched to the parking meter
lunges from his floppy ears
like a candle naked
to the wind.

Air. Water. Earth. Fire.

What spirit flames in things,
hurts our stone-like hands?

The two brown girls yanking the barking
puppy back up the street
cannot feel its heat,
may never feel it.

The Bible speaks of a burning bush
and its thunderous voice,
but I flare brighter
than the sun.

Air. Water. Earth. Fire.

The mix is fatal, combustible when flung
in the face of a man's
flickering fate, ashes
like snow in his
weeping eyes.

A click of a coin, the flash of scarlet
violations, start a roaring me
that can never be spent.

I am the breaker of laws,
human and sublime.

Autumn has no season in my faithless heart,
and I carry that mutt home
with a terrible laugh.

Fire. Fire. Fire. Fire.

DISCIPLE

I understand silence very well.
I mean, I understand what it does,
not what it is really,
if it really is.

I used to understand both,
what it is and what it does,
when I was still a child,
but growing up means losing it,
along with the rest.

I go back to being a child
sometimes, eating slippers and
reading ceiling cracks,
just for that reason,
to understand what silence is,
which is always what it is not,
at least now, but was then,
more than an idea,
less than a word.

The nun who expired from Sioux
arrows in her non-existent breasts
showed me it first,
                    slapping me hard enough
to see its incandescent fallout,
                    laughing at her bad breath.

Writing does not alter it,
nor does speaking
(even to yourself),
the unearthing of worms
for a few Egyptian dances,
not in the slightest,

sitting in a corner in the middle of the room,
playing with rosaries of ocean air
like jelly beans,

but who can tell for sure,
I mean, even then?

Hold yourself,
hold yourself down
at all frazzled edges
like a wind-raped sheet
and you will feel its shape.

And there was that old lady
with paper hair who flamed in her parlor
for three entire days
                              until my hands warmed
with it, and we skipped
(all three of us) around its
burnt marshmallow body.

I understand silence very well,
what it does, not what it was,
and, sometimes,
I am silence.

EGO

Does the atom mimic
the universe
or does the universe
mimic the atom?
It should not matter,
but it does, does matter.

There is a difference
of oceans
foamed between
Moby Dick's white spray
and the sneaky sperm
worming its way
to imitation.

When the whole world
revolves, we perch
like crows on the naked
limb of a root . . .

or is it that
a skull has swiveled
on its wire base?

Freud lies on a couch
and murmurs up at my
cellar's veined sky,
feeling the silence
like rich black soil
around his heart.

GAME

Who shall decide the rules?

Soundless and wordless,
make a move across the bed,
I love you like this,
a flower,
a water lily
folded in upon itself
(dripping crystal lights).

I will always love you
like this,
       a pudding-soft animal
of many liquid parts and peaks,
neb cushioned by cowskin,
fangs overflowing sheep,
vulva like a kitten
arching for my
glass rod
touches,

but you will not always be
like this,
       must become as distant
as a witch ranting at moons,
flaking off your twisted
trunk into hunched
piles of stars
like salt.

Who shall design the board,
its pieces and players?

Wittgenstein could not finish
his symphony either,
surrendered to silence,
marking notes on the night
with a divining chalk
that drew nothing
but a noose
of students
(scrubbed like beets)
for hanging his logic,

playing power games
from beginning to end,
while his love impaled its
ingrown heart upon the *A*'s
of the surrounding Alps.

I pump you full of myself, and
you curl back into cobra sleep.

Who shall say when it's over,
who wins or loses?

MONUMENT

Perhaps stasis, atoms
locked in a widowhood
of air to waterfalls,
prevents the rain
from sculpting tears,
memories of free, wild
years in a schoolyard
where the class bullies
nailed boys to the wall,
spelling out victory
over fear and growth
with obscene signs.

A concrete bench
squats in the dawn's
rain, forming another
dash in the iambic
line with other benches
around the courtyard,
which I must watch
out of fatigue, dank
boredom, fallen limbs
leaping at them like
talons from last night's
winter storm.

But they have no
names or real features,
no imagined voices,
and I cannot read their
tomb-gray messages,
feeling only dead pain,
lost forms.

UTOPIA

The silent sidewalk springs free
when I release it from its black
leash
    and curls into the tunnel
    under the A & P,
              like a worm
              on cellophane.

Skyscrapers split their bright sides,
spill out cookies and manholes
and salt
    and enough detergent
    to wash the city white,
              to bleed
              tomato cans.

I touch the face of a Protestant
pole vaulter, feel his cardboard
grimace
    of triumph melting into soup
    that scums itself
              around
              Walden Pond.

Bottles blow their tops like oil
wells at the ecstasy of my touch,
smearing
    the sky's brick walls
    with rivers of salmon
              and semen
              promises.

61

I walk on the waxed backs of wives
until their aprons open drawers
like wombs
            to the knife of No Sale,
            numbers branding their
                              flanks
                              in Clorox.

CAGE

Measure the silence
with minute hands,
tickle it along,
lock it in slots.
A dead man paces
his tiger cell
and dreams Greece.
The sun beats him
down with cymbals.

There can never be
absolute silence.
Listen. The blood
gurgles and pours
through limp pipes.
Ariel leaps on tin-
foil feet from end
to end, tingling.

I cannot escape
my self's vanity,
the crack of sun-
blistered fingers,
undulating hands
stuffing the coffin
with old sneakers
and bent beer cans.

LEGEND

I eat roots and ants
for survival, the acid
of dirt-haired feet
ripping at stomach
fears like saws.

> Mountains were once made
> from newspaper silence,
> cyclone-flattened towns,
> flesh cut to the knuckle,
> building parent absences
> into castle sounds.

My fingers bleed long
pus-ruffled ribbons
of a queen's red river-
run as I crawl across
this cake-dry land.

> Pencils became rapiers
> that lifted eyeballs
> out with wing-plashing
> ease, grappling shades
> on the crushed parlor rug
> alive with roses.

The pigeon parachutes
lightly to the creek bed
and pecks worms from mud,
but I tear off its head,
taste pin-feathers again.

Beauty was perfection
blue-frozen in a table's
dust-skated mirror,
husking me like corn
for owl-awe features
of an Iroquois mask.

I revenge myself on
grizzly bears, devour
raw hearts and claws
until my own roars
bring down the sky's
granite shoulders.

HIS

His infant lime impressed
to structure diamond cocks
from hens,
petrified and crystal wrens
strangled in golden boughs.

His sullen saints of sunlight
icy, caked and walking
past, past
the buried flower skulls

bootless high and cold.

SYNTAX

Steeple, spear, penis, mountain
shoots, stops, heaves, snows
on
love, hate, rain, song,
again and again,
a pivot
and piano
roll
pricked by art
into elaborate stairs
that tremble when I breathe,

a hub
and wheel of love
that crushes wheat nuggets
and silver chests
into grist
for the mills of men,
not gods,

a generator drum
that sends a tap root
streaking, screaming inside
the universal dark.

What is this,
this miracle I make,
if not the black-hand silence
after fact, when the man
presents his naked back
to the woman closing
around his pearl?

I believe, now, as silence mantles
her shoulders in neon petals
(a cream-poured softness
almost unimaginable)
that the time has
come to celebrate
silence
without recourse
to any vague
wildness
or burnt
offerings
of ragged nerves
at the trash can brink
where sailors fall off day.

The name
the names
the naming
the namings
the namings of lives
the namings of deaths
the namings of things and beings
is the pleasure most missed,
the settling of feathers
on stones and skeletons,
the letting of poison
out of clouds,
the sinking flings
at marble myths,
hissing like
acid kisses,

but it is a childhood pleasure,
sheerest infancy, when fingers
trailed off into cedars,

and the sun was apple
in a cobra mouth,
eating flowers,
crooning silk,
draining
hills,

a silence so sweet
it repels all bees
with an inhuman excess
and ripples a tragic mask
in a goathead's bleached grin,
snow-fired, cow-fat, reflecting
nothing but its curled mirror self.

My love, I touch, clutch a pillow,
squeeze a sigh from its down,
wondering what proud gander
was hanged from its own
doubting heart
for its fur
drippings,
silence,
always,
I love silence
more than you, more
than your guppy lips
bumping against neck muscles,
your bluejay beak digging down
between worn ship ribs
for the worm end
of me,
love it
for the vast nest
vacuum of its cave,
its pulsing
torch.

If you cannot see
the ordering eye,
let me love
where you
cease
to be,
the shape
of contentment
stretching over our bed
in a canopy of long breaths,
making the hairs on my chest
(still carved by your arm)
tingle like Phoenician
sails about to leap
above the wind,

so that
the doing starts,
and the doing becomes
what I never finished or
dared call by name,
genders
lost
in a whirlwind splash
of color
across rock faces,
frantic brush strokes
from a virgin's plucked hair
that waver like a carrousel
behind a closed mind,

reflexes of existence,
repetitions like moons
scratched in sand,
masturbating
time

into glass
figures of a girl
who lost her soul's sins,
the doing as automatic
as a brand-new toaster,
the order of chaos
disguised by syntax,

until order has a plan,
until order is poetic:

a rope of nuts,
a ring of charms,
a belt of small heads
that weep against steel thighs
as they pursue a behemoth evil thing
back into the sea.

I celebrate silence,
the naming and the doing,
but you must link the chain,
shut the door, lock the eye
in an asylum of revolving
bodies where heaven
has a place and
death no
power.

You are the architect primeval,
the objective case where I
lay my emptied head
on velvet breasts,
suckle silence,
give breath,
grab hold.

Flower, crib, cunt, factory
clears, comes, rests, takes
in
    idea, envy, lake, dirge,
again and again,
a womb
and roller
pin
urged by thumbs
into a cathedral stem
that blossoms when I inhale you,

a pie
and pit of love
that fuses split apples
and wooden saints
into food
for the minds of men,
not goddesses,

an earthquake gap
that swallows all machines
in an entropy of night
without name
or ghost.

ENDS

The beauty of this world
is that I survive and love it
like I do,
      although the room
in my mind where it lives
grows cold from the lack
of furniture and human heat,
as if the last barren stanza
must fill with infant feet
before the twilit doom can
lift free of rhyming ends.

It is forever silent here,
the space between breaths,
shadows crawling across me
like pen-fine lines of a
mother whose child is dead
of strange wounds,
          racking
my body not for love or hope,
but for the pity of departing
arts, the shape of failure's
gummy sacks, stone thighs
to colonnade the night.

The beauty of this world
is that I survive and love it
like I do,
      keeping it occupied.

✎ MOTHER ✎
AND CHILD

Loved heart, what can I say?
When I was a lark, I sang;
When I was a worm, I devoured.

—THEODORE ROETHKE

SAND

A sudden moon of grain
(still perfect)
             spilled
among neuter
rocks like a futile
              seed,

round as a ball,
less than a bead,
lacking a mouth
to serpent arcs
around love lost,
never restored.

I am the sun
              (itself)
briefly, blinking
at nothing near,
              contained
by my content
until I dare wink
              awake
diamond light,
weep alive someone
else's crystal eye
(I think),
suckling
the lilac sea
that never recedes
or washes free

this taste
of salt.

GRASS

Clump of dune weed
anchored to overturned
time
    by cables
of stubborn
hunger,
      made content
by survival
and impossible
berries.

Nothing has limit
(you see),
can be reaped again,
can be replanted
in stillness,
in air,
    grafted
to the wind
by my hair.

Eye to eye,
mother and child,

green comes to me,
crawls up my leg
like icy soda
in a straw,
      to kiss
      and enter
the jungle's
oven lips,

brined by water,
browned by the wind
that rips at me
without stop
or fire

until I fall,
roll free,
   flying away

in wheel
   upon wheel
of white
gulls.

TRASH

Uniform
       forgetting
which war
it last
fought,
     I scream and am
painted
brown
around
pain:

bald,
ancient,
safe cave
of the world:

man-made
and locked
into passion
for swallowing
debris:
      I sit and sit
in patient order
(holding silence so
close), sipping down
paper caskets and
twisted tanks
of a urine
courage:

steel law
is what I crave
and am,
      the hole
escape

from nature's
predator beaks.

I wait for ruins
of dead men
to descend
and end
my own
ruin,
          pivoting
stars
          in the vortex altar

that bleeds
a single
son.

SEA

Standing knee-high in its restless hands,
feeling stone knuckles tense with power,
kneading arms and legs,
melting thighs into strokes,
the sense, always, of a gigantic wave
(invisible as wind) about to collapse

on me, on me, the ocean must
be respected, if never loved,

as I stride closer to the cold currents
of its dark heart, ripping at seaweed
veins until warm Bermuda
blood gushes in around my
armored breasts, cupping them to shells,
as I am frozen fast to my pearl marrows,

star-fish stiff under taunts
of the sand-piper sunset,

shifting deeper into smothering breasts
(hair to hair, heart to heart), lapping
up the bitter milk scud like
a bitch, tasting earth's grit,
the pebble bottom of things and beings,
as I breathe in a squid's final semen:

curling, curdling in coral,
O scallion child again!

ᷜ Child ᷜ

PORCH

The infant mole
left as a gift
on the back
altar
invites prayer:

    tiny human hands
    still clenched
    in frantic
    efforts to claw
    themselves
    back into earth's
    black womb:

    fur body (smaller
    than a palm)
    still warm
    as sun-nuzzled
    pollen,
            perfect
    except for
    the punctured neck.

It is easy
to imagine its cry
of surprise
when

        GOD'S GREAT GRIN

struck home.

THRESHOLD

The baby in the carriage
blinks at him, smiles summer,
guppy fingers wiggling
through the haze
of a tidal sea.

"I will always love you!"
he shouts and plunges
the knife like a shark
through moth-wing nets,
leaving in his wake
one enormous nova.

ATTIC

Think of the mice
that squeak
corners
into accordion
dirges,
       gnawing
upon one another's
pink toes,

and of the fly
caught
by a ceiling
web, sucked
into a husk
for air
to whistle
down.

Think of the pines
hacked to death,
sawed in half,
sanded smooth,
nailed
to a cloud
for the comfort
of a human
hand,

and of the dust
that mounts
empty trunks and
mummy forms,
feces
of angels

and poet remains
intermingled
by decline.

Think of it all
under a tent
of wooden
screams
that smother
your breath
to her whisper.

BEDROOM

Familiar monsters
struggle
and grunt
in a linen dream
like gigantic
white corpuscles,
scaring you
near death.

See the fingers
hunch and slither
into night-grass
caves,
        searching
for a daisy heart
to light their
root way
to the secret
hoard,

being trapped
by the flood,
expelled
on shore,
        bloated
and bleached
                pale,
out of breath,
almost drowned.

See them fall
apart
before your
very eyes.

KITCHEN

Your mother murdered
calves and chickens
here,
      carved them
into cackling roasts
and giggling
breasts
        that tasted
of parchment
underwear,
              brownish
blood streaking
from your eyes
into the bowl
of bone
she held
(like a dentist)
at your chin
when you first
became ill,

and, as her hair faded
into old curtains,
she knitted you
a shroud
from the immaculate
table cloth
with her
finest silverware.

LIBRARY

Remember the stink
of saint and sinner
lives
    arranged
by alphabet
against the time
when rats
would tear them
from their
spines.

Remember:
        the word
grew out of the skull
of some forgotten
scholar
like a burning
soldier ant
        who makes
black sockets
dance
in rosy light.

Remember
the paragraphs
of lice
    that gathered
around your
grandfather's jowls
when he fell asleep
the last time,
his Bible
tumbling
to the floor

with the flutter
of broken
wings.

Remember, child,
the urine-scented hush
of shut windows
and hearts.

CELLAR

Roots leap
from your hand,
penetrate cement
and clay
with scalpel ease
in network
claws
that feel each
iron vein
for the pulse
of life,

surrounding them
until they sweat
a softer
earth.

You caress
the armadillo
spines of countless
beetles,
      squeeze
your own
rag faces
to the brink
of an explosion

out of fear
for self's
sudden
end.

HOME

Furniture shifts
blindly
       through
the dark house,
bumping against one
another,
       smashing
walls
with balled talons,
chairs unknitting
in furious
tendrils
       that creep
under locked doors.

Stay in the closet.
Sit still in the closet.
Hug your knees
like peeled apples
to your lips,
nibble at the night
until it fills
your eyes
       with light
enough to limn
your own
shadow.

Not a sob.
Not a word.
Not a sound
of fear or pain.
That is what they
feed on,

human
            excretions,
crushing
bones into milk
for their kitchen
machines.

❧ PERSONAE ❧

Lift them an elegy, poor you and I,
fair & strengthless as seafoam
under a deserted sky.

—JOHN BERRYMAN

THE BENCH SAYER

I listen to children
breaking one another,
as they break the hard earth,
and hear her ginghams overhead
rustle into flames
that tear away flesh.

     Autumn comes finally
     with whispers of bronze death,
     athletes wrenching the sun
     from my cloud-muscled heart
     and smashing it against slate fields
     until chestnuts moan, fall.

Sitting alone inside old age,
I wonder if the squirrels
will carry off her bones.

MUSEUM FELINE

Pinned in plaster to the floor,
she sat beside me,
the cat,
black and carved
green-eyed folds of fur
rubbing against my leg
with loving gestures
of her arrow head,
the cat,
cutting my leg's knee
until I fell,
then she licked away hair
and blunt nails,
kissing hands to bone,
and her teeth
were purring pearls . . .

PASSAGE
TO MANHATTAN

Sparrows pour through the haze
of bad dreams, seeding
leafless, lifeless roods
atop the drifted tombs
with their own soft selves,
as the dawn's gold yolk
breaks in his glassy hair,

our father who walks
upon concrete seas
for us, for us,

breaking daisy chains
against money-green knees
for us, for us,

before the descent,
devils breaking, too,
beneath his steel toes,

while mists, like myths,
like ragged children
dance, weeping, around
his stalking form, scattered
by his neatness,
his mad eyes.

INCANTATION AGAINST
HORROR FILMS

Children of the night
sup upon yourselves if you
want to unchain Dracula's moon.

Seeping through the bedroom wall
like a shadow with real fangs,
he assumes a father's drunken
gait, bends to kiss my cold
cheek, his breath like unearthed
tombs, his fingers wiggling
into faggots to fumble
at my throat,

and his victim in the madhouse
next door has my mother's laugh,
those cresting, bulging eyes
breaking into light when
her master's heavy body
anchors her to stone,
naked feet folded
into owl horns
to puncture
my raving
heart.

STILL LIFE

Unaware
of enraged suns
pounding at locked
claws, bats (not
necessarily vampires)
hang like downy
fruit from sea-cold
eaves of a secret
lair, drip, plump
and dusk-gray,
in contented
mass,

unaware, too,
of willows breaking
delicate
toes
against
their slate darkness.

They sleep
without sound
and refuse recognition
to the wind's
sway
until
reversals
turn their world,

then emerge
as screams
from the slack jaws
of night,
dribbled into flight

by deep repose
and ancient yearnings
for the moon's
pale blood.

MUSSOLINI

Hung, hog-thick, from
a meat hook's question
(beside his raw mistress),
blood rolling from his
eyes and torn-loose mouth
like unleashed garnets,

> why had my grandmother
> loved him so? was he the fire-
> haired son she lost to America
> in his twenty-third year,
> the one she always wrapped
> around her ski-slope shoulders
> like a mourning shawl?

cara mia, she used to pray
over the rosary of his name,
root fingers like Michelangelo's
when they clawed nimble David
out of his marble grave,
cara mia, cara mia, a chunk
of white heart whispering
across the black pan:

> he dangled upside down,
> bright as a giant sperm
> in the glossy photos,
> glinting like a shark
> before the sun bites
> through its silver veil.

LOBOTOMY OF LOVE
An Imperfect Canzone

FOR THE MUTILATED LADIES
FOUND UNDER THE DUNES
AT CAPE COD, 1969

Slow, remote, sure-handed with experience,
    the black-flowered archeologists
    resurrect almond dancers from another old urn
    my petal heart cannot restore, while fiddler crabs
    and ungainly gulls squabble, laughing, over
    the human debris of a lawless deity. Like
    the cold skeletons of rue Aristotle whittled
    from less tragic bones, beauty, too, is broken down

into proper proportions, again undone
    at its blood-mortared seams. "Each piece of flesh
    showed the marks of human teeth," marble-pure priests
    lie to imitate our prayers, the paradox
    of American art that moved his tidy mind
    and taxiderming blade to remove their hearts.

ECOLOGY

The quick pleasure of a child
remains in what he is not.

Skies bleed themselves awake
only when the earth has turned away.

Trees bend to us, bend to the wind,
but retain their defiant thrust.

Myself a child, I saw my first dead
child in a leafless living room.

Under concrete and tar, the earth
breathes through filigree of worms.

A casket crumbles and flesh rots.
The child returns (whole) in the sun.

MONA LISA

Hung in a Room Over
The Shannon Bar & Grill

The shaft of light
wormed her stomach
to the bottom bone
of her beginning break
into darkness and life.

"This is the truth,"
light damned her, biting her.

Shrouded river
skeletons heard her
through woolen miracles,
she breathed steam pockets,
my goodness, yes, tearing

helicopters of dust,
rotating worlds.

In the black flesh
under me, men
are smothered blind,
                          she smiled
an inch-wide light, pulsing
through lace-wounded windows,

a flicker sign of songs
owled from neon oooooo's,
sold moons, swollen,
cover, cover
yourself, your selves,
she laughed and fractured light.

"Stop lying," light
warned to confuse
blacks and whites,

double imaged
like the Father Frost
of poets grown cold
under ground, spectacles like
goggles in the flames.

Felt braids of light
fell from her,
                out of her

star-stitched teeth
and cathedral womb.
The lights oozed from her
and slipped into their moon
(pretended demise, but

she refused
them burial), snaking

from her dumb lips
on the legs of flies.

LEAVING THE OLD NEIGHBORHOOD

I

Leaf-bent wounds heavy
with rain, bleeding from time
to time, I arched slender maples
into golden wheels

and the sun rolled down, pierced
by the hour of my nine,

my tear-soft hands shaping a plot.

II

Like a black number
I crawled inside the rose
and lay, naked and shivering,
in her fiery song

as each Japanese note
feathered a hollow bone

for my yearning heart to shaft.

III

Winter came and blasted dew
into brittle crystals,
turning the rose around, around,
a diamond without doors.

The tough vowel of the rose
echoes my shell's one cry.

We are sick to death of dying.

SUMMER SONATA

Sun-struck
petals like burnt babies
curling on the sill,
the specific rose
blooms once, an explosion
of blood, then rots
back to the black night
that once suckled
its thorny worm.

Crumpled
naked on the wood floor
like a bridal sheet,
the gray-haired woman
is stiller than the fly
buzzing at her
open eyes, the knife
that crucified
her flock-free thighs.

I am
the sun. I burn and fall.
Electric signs blink,
break underfoot like screams,
Van Gogh's weary shoes.
I swim among
snakes, father, and eat
God's red eye blind.
O, I sink to stone!

SAY HELLO
TO PURGATORY

The old lady rode the elevator
like a dotty, dainty queen.

White-slippered toes curled,
gripped the morning's steel edge
as we fell through grave-dark
layers of a brainless beast.

Two husbands gone to seed
in plots of her Bible-stern eyes.

Three sons fled her narrow hips.

She plummets with a cat smile
that serpents my own, down,
slipping through the slot
of her empty mail box.

ARCTIC GRACE

I

Like an iceberg, groaning and
growing from its mirror self,
the mind moves slowly into winter.

Innocent of seasons, ghostly herds
of bison congeal their desperate
breath into downy fields,

billowing water lilies at each
root shot, the first sharp fang,
become a mammoth dancing bear

chained by golden hordes of naked
Indians, mountain and foothills
to the frozen-mad sea.

II

Behind window frosts, arterial
philosophies harden with hoary age
into the arthritic talons

of graveyard spinsters, ripping
aside icy snow to slash at dawn's
grim pregnancies, keening long winds

through their black and spindle
boughs like the singing corn silks
of their own floral-patterned pasts,

*the hunched, erect and flyer
contaminated, so elaborately frail,
by tissue, blood and being.*

Like an iceberg, groaning and
growing from its mirror self,
the mind moves so slowly into winter.

111

THE AGE DEMANDED AN IMAGE
A Villanelle for Ezra Pound

I
A blue carring was oldern tocsins.
  Young poettes exaulted
like red dancers from his open shirt.
  In the womb-robber's rose,
he smelt another wimin's cigar ash.

   Full lume through the Punic seas,
   I surge my alba petals.

Oriental luster
rubbed the old tub of guts wrong.
Titans he shaped in Europe's forge,
  woilds, like pomes, rocked between his knees.

"I need an official organ"—
  Khr-r-ist sat stiff as blood-dried braid
upon a murdered queen's breast,
  the Irish book worm, frailer than grass,
gently lilyed
  in his cool, calloused claws,
along with the others gathered
  for planting,
slender and green, in the cracks he made.

   Full lume through the Punic seas,
   I surge my alba petals.

He never knew: the selfish grace,
solitary ponds
  where his beetle mittens might not skate.
And broke her antique chair.

112

"Have all the sailors darkened?"

Time would drink of my alba.
Fragments, it moun now seam,
    or shrouds for his wind passions.

II
(The vortex is the white image!
In their own fat mirrors,
he drowned more than one.

Bastids stood his genius,
but nobuddy
was ever shur

when he crucified lines,
        exergue years, I iz yr.)

III
Erectus still, he rots—
        in coitus with song.
Dante knew what hell was:
"gran sacco che fa merda."
        Pound's fahrting devils prick him yet.

✌ THREE THEORIES ✌
OF FIELD COMPOSITION

What does it mean to know what a game is? What does it mean, to know it and not be able to say it? Is this knowledge somehow equivalent to an unformulated definition?

—LUDWIG WITTGENSTEIN

SEMANTICISM

I love seasons.

I love the season, the seasonal sway
of color and form,
                    not so much
for its tangible sap,
the syrup-scented blood
of steel restraint
                    (diluting ovals
                    to richer zeros)

though that has its sentient pleasure,
though that has its sensuous refrains:

harsh, leather-brown bark being ripped
down into cameo snows by the satin
antlers of a spider
                    tumbling
                            bones
                                 like
                                    naked
                                         sinners
into summer's
rose-thorn flames:
                    plaster milk,
                    molten dust,
                    sudden airs
sucked
        from heaven's luscious heaps
        of gray upon gray bodies,
                            bouquet and bodice
                            of sullen ashes
untinctured by Italian psalms,
untouched by Italian palms,

                                        salt embers
                                        of a pollen
                                        desire
                                                to FLARE
flowers into resurrections,
attenuated autumn flocks atom-bombing
from a global urn,
                        expressions, my love,
                        of seminal relief,
sun-burnished lover arms
like cypress roots
                        lipping seeds,
                        stitching stars,
                        uniting universes
in a languid rainbow lullabye,
                        consuming night,
                        consecrating all:

a moan of winter
overheard:

not even for this: its fecund images:

stone toe and
rusty talon
                for whatever velvet ideal
                has survived childhood
                                        diseases,
dreamy old love murders, books
of militant woes, wary worms,
                                easy
                                compound
                                allegories
of leaf-fat youth and frost-thin age,
life and death phrases smoothing down
symbol-gnarled rivers, symbol-stuffed corpses,

risen banks,
hanging trees,
mountain flocks
phoenix flights,

the suicide of gods
            and their raucous idioms
            of armoured
                    rue, rue, rue:

twilight sighs
            shushing awake infant-pink dawns,
seven stages
of mankind myths
mouthed by bad actors,
                lapping plows into spears,
                chewing sperms into chains,

whole complexes of cherry Christs
like childhood's paper lollipop parade,
                      featherless
yellow, yarrow stalks
            scratching
                masks of dolor
in
  virgin
      dust:
         O

       NO

I love the steel reason outside it!
I love the machine gears inside it!

           the pure idea of it
           the pure good of it

the pure evil of it
the absolute and
implacable wheel

of its coming and its going,
of its going and its coming,
                    the icy mind
behind its blind mole paws
fumbling at leaf order in the alien winds,
packing black space vacuums
into Madonna ovaries
with silver limbs,
                    slipping into an onion
moon,
        long potato fuses
                    BLASTING
                              tunnels
                                 of
                                eyes
in the soft-bodied, peach-bellied coal

where ships break
                    apart,
                            whales heave
and leave
their
ribs
    in luminous maps,
                        white traces
                        of an
                                acid
                                    art.

SENTIMENTALISM

See an old man, dirty as soil sin,
be more precise, alligator skin
like an ill-fitting shirt (archaic, that),
bunched at the neck, splotched
with baby lungs that wail
at each painful release,
                scrawny birch sapling
                leaping in an ostrich
                stroke
                    between
the pair of mounted tusks,
                yellowed and honed
by the strop of a woman's
                tongue,
frayed, I say, by apple-slicers from mother
Eve's fantasy factory.

See the tremble in his crowning hands,
vein impressions of barren boughs,
birdless black,
                fleshed, perhaps, with ancient
                parchment designs, hermetic as
                a Northwest Passage to vague
                new lands,
                    a lost Oriental kite
                    (I like that,
no end),
            filtered for smoking the charcoal
of his collapsed years
as they seek
            the earth peace of woolen pants
insanely wrinkled at his empty pouch and crotch,
nervously furrowing fists into knots
of remembered fights,

a forgotten artist
flayed bare
by fear.

See the eyes, jewels still (I demand it!),
cloudy though, glass stoppers
for the acid sorrow within,
obtuse too, yes, but not
                          obsolete, romantic as
                          all hell in there,
turfs of lifeless, greenless grass,
a frozen field of knives and pricks,
you fools, my skeletal lovelies,
walking me into summer,
                          cast adrift,
                          actually,
atop a flaking skull
in an empty village,
                    cannibal-fine,
                    cannibal-sharp,
                    cannibal-clean

as Gibraltar's bird-beaked gates,
snowed by the cold ways
of the wide world

                    into the brute silence
                    of not thinking self:

wanting only the stripping sun
to bend, to kneel, to kiss
his once-candied lips
into a moan
of content-
ment,

furry as a purr
below rawer shouts
and more studied hymns,

slippery
as the sibilant
serpent salvation
of a fatal womb,
its night-still
pivot,

bud

of a husked
grasshopper humming
batteries of shit flies
shafting

mama.

SERPENTISM

Survival, my love.

Sucking on the stem
of a simulated rose,
    I breathe it in,
    swallow its flames,
one by one,
   to become
      the diamond snake pattern
      that governs dawn's naked
thigh stars,
selfishly seeking
     a moment's stone cellar,
     darkness and felt life,
wet bodies and
lioness legs wrapping their icy grave joy
around my bag of sadness.

       Petals, white,
       petals
white as fleece,
white as fleeced bones,
white as water-lily beds,
white as hospital sheets
     for the mangled mole
     murdered in his mother's hole
     by a playful priest
     and pious cat
     tongues.

Shed a tear, two.
Release the rosary
of bubble mendacities
that bind our drowned son

until my own dead-man lips
can sip and surround
his amino acid sea.

                    Vines, too,
                        vines
torn from a theatre
balcony, fragments of a rope ladder
now stiffer than sticks,
                    pieces of stale tail
to braid into a cable noose
                        for every feather
                        legend that ever
tickled art's fancy.

Sleep, sleep and sift gold-tooth smiles
from the swan-breasted ashes,
                        if you must,
an elegant finger bone
                    (scholar lean)
and its Japanese
                ring,
                    bell and candle
curled around
my book's blackest similes.

                        Autumn comes in.
                        Autumn comes in bleeding:
an abstract splash
of senseless
scarlet
                    rags,
                    like flags,
                    like napkin flags.

Simpering sycophant of natural phenomena
(to my friends), I murder no less
the milk in my refrigerator mind,
the meat in my mortal chest,
still ripe
and still hot
with expectations of another summer feast.